Bandits & Outlaws

© Aladdin Books Ltd 1995

Designed and produced by
Aladdin Books Ltd
28 Percy Street
London W1P 0LD

First published in 1995 in the United States by
Copper Beech Books, an imprint of
The Millbrook Press
2 Old New Milford Road
Brookfield, Connecticut 06804

Design
David West Children's
Book Design
Designer
Flick Killerby
Editor
Jim Pipe
Picture Research
Brooks Krikler Picture Research
Illustrators
McRae Books, Florence, Italy

Printed in Belgium

Library of Congress Cataloging-in-Publication Data

Ross, Stewart.
Bandits and outlaws / Stewart Ross ; illustrated by McRae
Books.
p. cm. -- (Fact or fiction)
Includes index.
Summary: Examines a number of noted outlaws in
history, including Robin Hood, Jesse James, and Bonnie
and Clyde.
ISBN 1-56294-649-8 (lib.bdg.)
1-56294-189-5 (pbk.)
1. Outlaws--History--Juvenile literature. [1. Robbers and
outlaws--History.] I.Title. II. Series: Ross, Stewart. Fact
or Fiction.
HV6441.R67 1995   95-13146
364.1'092'2--dc20   CIP   AC

FACT *or* FICTION:

Bandits & Outlaws

Written by *Stewart Ross*
Illustrated by *McRae Books, Italy*

COPPER BEECH BOOKS
BROOKFIELD, CONNECTICUT

CONTENTS

INTRODUCTION

Have you ever dreamed of being a bandit? Have you ever wondered what it would be like to get away from dull, everyday things and live in the wild, amid danger and constant excitement?

The word "bandit" conjures up such romantic images – colorful thieves, smugglers, and highwaymen; daring and heroic figures robbing the rich to feed the poor; champions of the oppressed; outcasts dedicated to taking their rough but honest revenge on an unjust society.

Think again!

You have in mind the bandits of fiction – Robin Hoods, all smiles and bravado. Forget such figures! They exist only in novels and movies.

History's real bandits were never so pleasant. They were usually vicious criminals. They robbed the rich, but very rarely did they give to the poor. They shunned the law, and in its place they set up their own brutal law, based on violence, theft, and murder.

This book will reveal the truth. You will discover how the noble bandit is the creation of the storytellers and ballad writers. And you will enter the evil world of the true bandit – and be glad that you have been there only in your dreams!

BANDITTO!

There have been criminal gangs in every country since the beginning of history. But "bandits," the word we use to describe them, did not enter the English language until 400 years ago. It came from the Italian *banditto*, meaning outlaw, a person banned from society.

Almost at once, people began objecting to the word. "Banditti do you call them?" snorted one English gentleman. "I am sure we call them plain thieves in England!" From the start, it seems, bandits were seen as different from common criminals. Their romantic-sounding name made their crimes seem less wicked!

"Bandit" became an umbrella word, covering thieves, outlaws, brigands, smugglers, and highwaymen (*below*). Only rarely was it used for urban evil-doers. The bandit was linked to the country, with gangs hiding from the law and robbing travelers. The Robin Hood image arose because some bandits really had been cheated. They were outcasts, and a few, like the Greek klephts, really did fight against tyranny.

A Modern Bandit (above)
Phoolan Devi, the Indian "Bandit Queen," was banished from her village when she was raped by men of a higher caste.

As leader of a bandit gang, she became a champion of the poor. She is now a politician.

Song Dynasty, Chinese bandits

John Bixley, English smuggler

Rob Roy, Scottish cattle thief

Prince of Thieves
Kevin Costner starred in this modern version of the Robin Hood story.

BANDITS OF FICTION. Robin Hood (page 18), Jesse James (page 38), the Outlaws of the Marsh (page 12), Ned Kelly (page 42), Rob Roy (page 30) – there are bandit stories in every age and culture – their appeal to novelists and filmmakers is obvious.

Bandits led action-packed lives, fighting, chasing, hiding, and escaping. They were colorful, romantic characters, too – the brilliant archer in love with the dazzling Maid Marion, the young lad deadly with the six-gun, the outlaw in an iron mask. Each one of them is a storyteller's dream!

Many modern stories and films are based on tales from the past, so remember that although in popular myth bandits brought bullies to justice, in real life it was usually the bandits who were the bullies!

Bandit stories are popular all over the world – from songs of Dick Turpin (top right), to reports of Mexican bandits and smuggling (middle and bottom right).

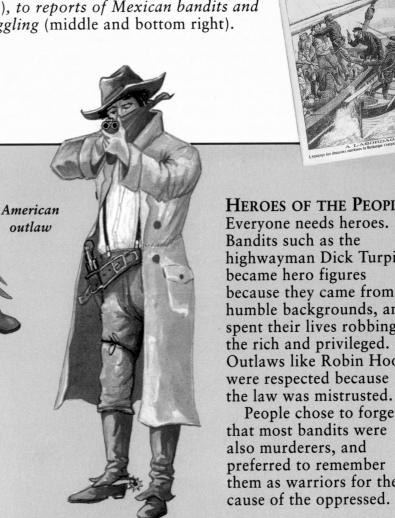

American outlaw

18th-century highwayman

HEROES OF THE PEOPLE

Everyone needs heroes. Bandits such as the highwayman Dick Turpin became hero figures because they came from humble backgrounds, and spent their lives robbing the rich and privileged. Outlaws like Robin Hood were respected because the law was mistrusted.

People chose to forget that most bandits were also murderers, and preferred to remember them as warriors for the cause of the oppressed.

CLASSICAL BANDITS

Few men and women chose to become bandits. Normally they took to banditry because they were outcasts from society, forced into crime because they had no other way of supporting themselves.

In the early European civilizations, one of the largest groups of outcasts was runaway slaves. Spartacus was a Greek robber of the first century B.C. When he was captured, he was not executed but sold to a gladiator school at Capua in southern Italy.

In 73 B.C., Spartacus and seventy others managed to escape. They set up a base on Mount Vesuvius, and runaway slaves from all over Italy joined them. Spartacus had about 90,000 in his unruly gang. But after four years of terrorizing Italy, he was defeated by the Roman General Crassus.

Hadrian's Wall, England, built by the Romans to keep out raiders from the north.

SPARTACUS. One of the most famous of all bandits, he became a legend in his own lifetime.

Since his death, his story has been retold many times. It has all the elements of a good bandit tale – the struggle of a brave and heroic figure against the forces of tyranny. The best-known Spartacus film casts Kirk Douglas as the bandit leader (*left*).

NO MERCY!

The Romans did not deal with bandits lightly – Spartacus and most of his followers were crucified.

The Romans hoped that the sight of thousands of men strung up along the roads would serve as a deterrent to any would-be bandits and runaways.

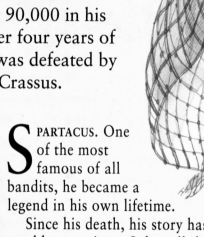

Learning to Kill
The most horrible aspect of the gladiator school was knowing that you might have to kill a fellow student.

TARGET – CARAVAN!

Between about 600 B.C. and 100 B.C. a remarkable trade route ran between Syria and China, crossing 2,500 miles of mostly barren terrain. Bags of gold and silver were exchanged in the east for valuable silks, spices, and jewels. Inevitably, such precious goods were obvious targets for bandit gangs.

The most dangerous bandits came from Dzungaria, a region north of China. Chinese emperors occasionally sent forces against them. But most of the time merchants had to protect themselves by traveling in caravans (heavily-guarded groups, *below*).

EARLY ROBBER GANGS

Robber gangs flourished in prosperous areas like China, India, Italy, and the Middle East. Jesus set his story about the Good Samaritan on the Jerusalem-Jericho highway because of the road's dangerous reputation. Further east, large robber gangs terrorized India, some killing their victims in religious rituals.

Syrian

Bulla's 600-strong gang rampaged around Italy for almost two years in the third century A.D. "Feed your slaves," he told the Roman authorities, "and they won't become bandits!"

Early Bandits

Roman   *Indian*   *Chinese*

9

BANDIT GANGS OF ANCIENT CHINA

For many centuries, China was the bandit capital of the world. This was partly due to the difficulty of controlling such a large country and partly because natural disasters brought millions of people to the verge of starvation. Many turned to crime to survive.

Banditry reached its height during the last century of the Tang Dynasty (618–907 A.D.). Well-organized bands under leaders such as Huang Ch'ao were more like armies than bandit gangs. For years, they roamed the country, terrorizing the people, robbing merchants (*above*), and openly defying the government. Wang Chien even formed his own bandit state, but insisted on keeping his old nickname: "Wang-pa the Thief!" Other gangs raided ships on the canals (*below*).

HUANG CH'AO, BANDIT EMPEROR

Hsi-tsung (*below*) became emperor at the age of twelve. Although he was a lively lad, his charm did not last. He developed into a vicious and incompetent emperor.

Banditry flourished under his weak leadership.

The crisis came in 880 A.D. Huang Ch'ao's bandit army drove the emperor from his capital at Chang' an (see map, *far right*).

Huang Ch'ao tried to set himself up as emperor. He failed, but it was a year before Hsi-tsung got his city back!

The Wang Ming
Chinese bandits (above) *were often mounted to ensure a quick getaway. They were known as the "Wang Ming," meaning "those who had abandoned their village and family."*

RIVERS OF LIFE

China's civilization (*above*) grew up around great rivers, notably the Yangtze and the Huang Ho, and the canals built by the Tang and later dynasties. They provided water for the rice fields and were the principal highways between the country's interior and the eastern seaboard. But flooding was a common disaster, forcing many to seek a living through robbery.

THE PERIOD OF THE TEN STATES

— rivers
canals
The Great Wall

Chang'an

Yangtze

Liangshan marshes

Huang Ho

South China Sea

Collapse of Tang Dynasty. *This followed soon after the rebellions of the 870s, leaving a variety of smaller states (above). This proved a golden era of opportunity for bandits.*

OUTLAWS OF THE MARSH

Where could you meet with Black Whirlwind, Marvelous Traveler, and Ten Feet of Steel Hu? In medieval China, among the lofty mountains rising above the Liangshan Marsh, in Shandong province. They are heroes of *Outlaws of the Marsh* (or *The Water Margin*), one of the great bandit tales.

The novel was written by Shi Nai'an, who witnessed massive peasant unrest during the fall of the Yuan Dynasty, and based his stories on the activities of real-life bandits. Outlaw leader Song Jiang and his followers fought for honesty and fair government under the slogans "Pursue the Way of Heaven!" and "Wipe out Tyranny!"

Shi tells of the formation of the bandit gang under its 108 glorious officers (seven are shown *below*), its battles with corrupt officials (notably the wicked Gao Qiu), and its betrayal. The adventures of the bandits, officials, gentry (*above*), and peasants are described with humor and great detail. When they are finally overcome, the reader is left in no doubt about who the real criminals were – not the Outlaws of the Marsh!

Cai Xing
(Lone Flower)

Duan Jing Zhu
(Golden Hair Dog)

Lin Chong
(Tiger's Head)

*O*UTLAWS OF THE MARSH was so popular that its sequel was banned by the Qing dynasty rulers as they thought it might encourage a peasant revolt!

During the Ming and Qing dynasties, over 48 different plays were written using themes from the original story, and today dozens of local operas use characters from the book (*left*). So this work of fiction may well have encouraged generations of real bandits!

Hero of the Marsh Nicknamed the Marvelous Traveler (right), Dai Zong could amble 240 miles a day!

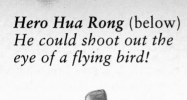

Hero Hua Rong (below)
He could shoot out the
eye of a flying bird!

REBELLIOUS TALES. Many of the tales used by Shi Nai'an in *Outlaws of the Marsh* came from the time of the Song Dynasty (960-1279). By the 12th century, the dynasty was beginning to lose power and there was widespread rebellion and banditry. Taking advantage of this, the Mongols, a tough, warlike people from the north, conquered China by 1279. Under Kublai Khan, and then Genghis Khan (*right*), they remained in power until 1367. This change in leadership had little effect on the mass of peasants, however, and China was soon plagued by bandits again.

HEAVEN'S MANDATE
A ruling Chinese dynasty was said to hold power through "Heaven's Mandate" (or blessing). To oppose it was to oppose the way of Heaven. This did not mean that a dynasty stayed in power forever. Sometimes a series of disasters, such as floods, coincided with unrest and widespread banditry. This was a sign that a dynasty's Mandate might be coming to an end, and rebellion was justified.

Zheng Tian Shou
(Pale Face)

Zou Run
(One Horn Dragon)

Sun Xin
(Little Yuchi)

Tong Meng
(Big Oyster)

RISINGS AGAINST THE MONGOLS
Revolts began in 1335. To make matters worse, in the 1350s eastern China was devastated by floods. To many Chinese it was now clear that the Yuan Dynasty had forfeited Heaven's Mandate.

Chu Yuan-chang emerged as the principal rebel leader. Overcoming his rivals in 1368, he set up a dynasty of his own – the Ming. Within 20 years, the Ming had driven out the Mongols, and to keep them out, fortified the Great Wall (*left*). The Ming's chief task was now to drive out banditry and get the country back on its feet.

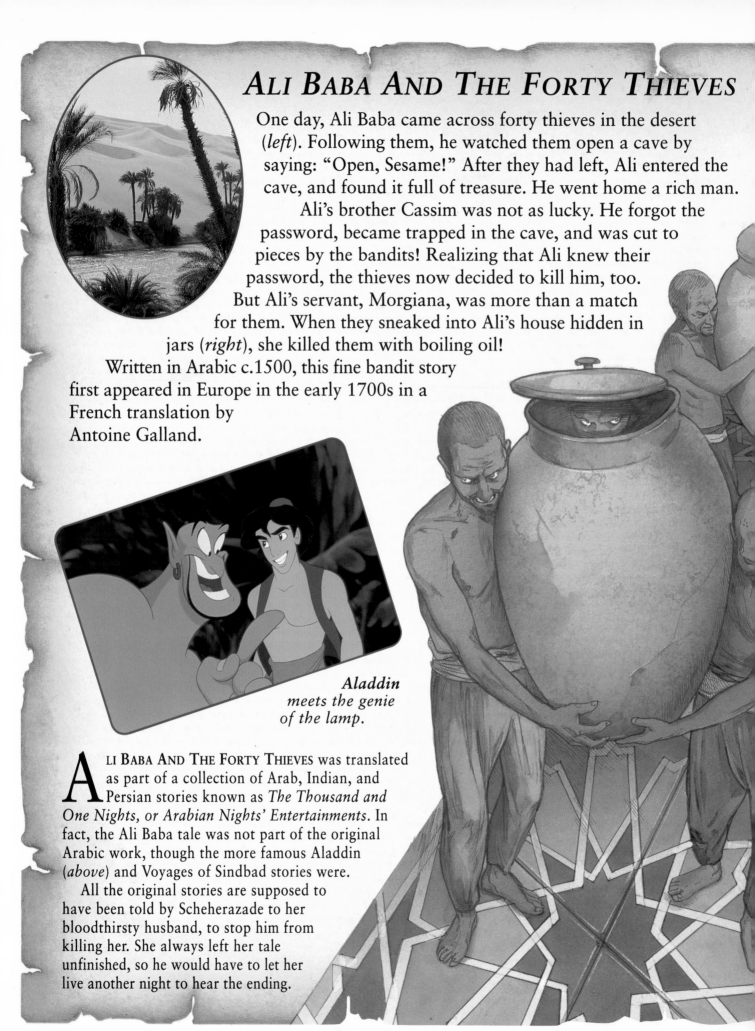

ALI BABA AND THE FORTY THIEVES

One day, Ali Baba came across forty thieves in the desert (*left*). Following them, he watched them open a cave by saying: "Open, Sesame!" After they had left, Ali entered the cave, and found it full of treasure. He went home a rich man.

Ali's brother Cassim was not as lucky. He forgot the password, became trapped in the cave, and was cut to pieces by the bandits! Realizing that Ali knew their password, the thieves now decided to kill him, too.

But Ali's servant, Morgiana, was more than a match for them. When they sneaked into Ali's house hidden in jars (*right*), she killed them with boiling oil!

Written in Arabic c.1500, this fine bandit story first appeared in Europe in the early 1700s in a French translation by Antoine Galland.

Aladdin
*meets the genie
of the lamp.*

ALI BABA AND THE FORTY THIEVES was translated as part of a collection of Arab, Indian, and Persian stories known as *The Thousand and One Nights, or Arabian Nights' Entertainments*. In fact, the Ali Baba tale was not part of the original Arabic work, though the more famous Aladdin (*above*) and Voyages of Sindbad stories were.

All the original stories are supposed to have been told by Scheherazade to her bloodthirsty husband, to stop him from killing her. She always left her tale unfinished, so he would have to let her live another night to hear the ending.

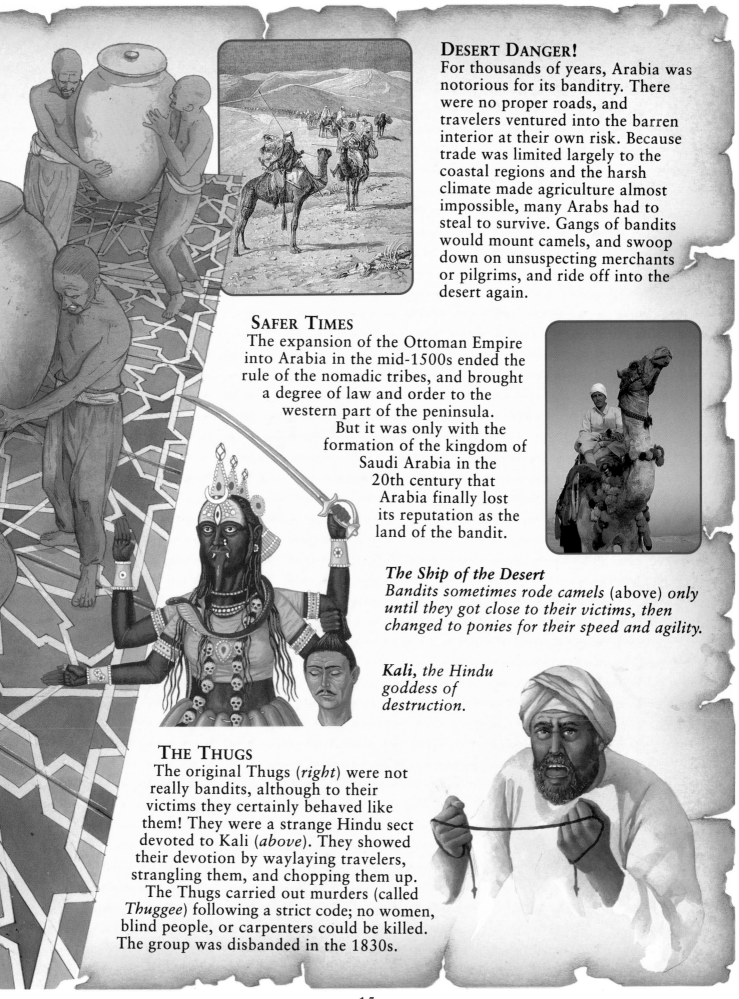

DESERT DANGER!

For thousands of years, Arabia was notorious for its banditry. There were no proper roads, and travelers ventured into the barren interior at their own risk. Because trade was limited largely to the coastal regions and the harsh climate made agriculture almost impossible, many Arabs had to steal to survive. Gangs of bandits would mount camels, and swoop down on unsuspecting merchants or pilgrims, and ride off into the desert again.

SAFER TIMES

The expansion of the Ottoman Empire into Arabia in the mid-1500s ended the rule of the nomadic tribes, and brought a degree of law and order to the western part of the peninsula.

But it was only with the formation of the kingdom of Saudi Arabia in the 20th century that Arabia finally lost its reputation as the land of the bandit.

The Ship of the Desert

Bandits sometimes rode camels (above) only until they got close to their victims, then changed to ponies for their speed and agility.

Kali, the Hindu goddess of destruction.

THE THUGS

The original Thugs (*right*) were not really bandits, although to their victims they certainly behaved like them! They were a strange Hindu sect devoted to Kali (*above*). They showed their devotion by waylaying travelers, strangling them, and chopping them up.

The Thugs carried out murders (called *Thuggee*) following a strict code; no women, blind people, or carpenters could be killed. The group was disbanded in the 1830s.

BANDITS FOR HIRE

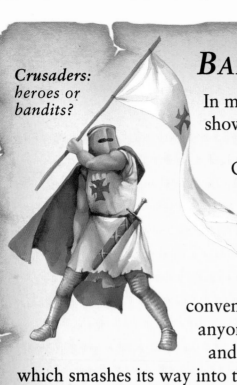

Crusaders: heroes or bandits?

In medieval Europe, banditry was part of everyday life, as shown in this story based around Poitiers, France, in 589 A.D. In the Convent of the Holy Cross, the princesses Clotild and Basina are furious that Abbess Leubovera isn't showing them enough respect. So they complain to the authorities and hire a gang of bandits (*main picture*). When a church emissary arrives and tells the ladies to behave, the gang beats him up!

The Abbess is now trapped within her own convent. The bandits seize the land, making short work of anyone in their way. The following spring, Clotild and Basina recruit a larger gang, which smashes its way into the convent. Leubovera is captured. But the princesses argue and the violence spreads. Eventually, royal forces arrive and the brigands are either killed or run back to the woods from which they had first come.

KNIGHTS IN SHINING ARMOR?

The Crusaders are often portrayed as honorable, God-fearing knights (*above*) – but in reality some were little more than bandits. The People's Crusade, led by Peter the Hermit in 1096, looted, raped, and murdered its way across Europe as local people refused to provide food.

Many knights went on the Crusades for financial reasons – the journey to the Holy Land provided plenty of opportunity for looting and it also had the blessing of the Pope! Kings also welcomed the Crusades as it meant unruly and rebellious knights were sent far from home.

Clotild and Basina

It was not unusual for wealthy women to escape from violent society in the peace and comfort of a convent. But Abbess Leubovera took on more than she bargained for when the Princesses Clotild and Basina joined her convent (below).

SANCTUARY

The Church stood for civilized behavior in the violent medieval world. An important example of this was *sanctuary*. Accused criminals could hide from the law inside a church or churchyard, where no violent act was supposed to take place. But, as the murder, in 1170, of Archbishop Thomas à Becket in Canterbury Cathedral, England showed, sanctuary was no guarantee of safety (*right*).

Robber Barons

Not all bandits were poor – gangs of knights could loot, kidnap, and murder, and still gain a King's Pardon. Law courts run by the local sheriff also turned a blind eye to such injustice, making the sheriff a hated figure (as in Robin Hood).

NASTY, BRUTISH, AND SHORT

Life in medieval Europe was generally nasty, brutish, and short. Apart from priests, all men carried arms and were expected to serve their lord in battle.

Those failing to obey a summons to court might be outlawed. Once outside the law, they could be killed without fear of prosecution. Bands of outlaws – poachers, thieves, vagrants, murderers, and rapists – could be found in every country.

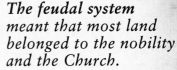

The feudal system *meant that most land belonged to the nobility and the Church.*

Peasants were forced to live off small strips of land, and a bad harvest or harsh taxes could leave thousands on the verge of starvation (above), *with little hope but charity (left). Not surprisingly, many were tempted to turn to crime.*

ROBIN HOOD

Who has not heard of Robin Hood? He has acquired such fame that today all kind-hearted bandits are known as "Robin Hoods." And yet no one even knows who the real Robin Hood was, or even if he existed at all.

A document of 1239 mentions a Yorkshireman described as "Robert Knight, outlaw." Tales of Robin the outlaw were circulating by the mid-13th century, and the first written reference appears in the poem *Vision of Piers Plowman* (1378).

In the early poems, printed more than a century later, Robin is more like a real medieval bandit. He kills bloodily and enjoys it. Slaying Guy of Gisborne, he sticks his head on the end of his bow! But with time, as more characters were added (*above*) by writers like Sir Walter Scott (in the novel *Ivanhoe*), Robin was transformed into the romantic figure we recognize today.

THE MERRY MEN. Robin Hood stories became popular because they satisfy people's needs – ordinary men and women can triumph over privileged and corrupt masters.

Robin's adventures have been turned into dozens of movies (*above*), most of which have little to do with the rough life of the medieval bandit!

The People's Champion?
In medieval poems about Robin Hood (below), there is little about robbing the rich and giving to the poor. He is far more concerned with fighting the evil sheriff's men and poaching the King's deer.

Bandits of the day might wear woolen breeches and a rough tunic – certainly not the thin green tights of Hollywood's Merry Men!

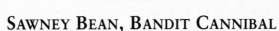

SAWNEY BEAN, BANDIT CANNIBAL
By no means did all outlaws become heroes, and certainly not Sawney Bean (1394–1437), who lived in a set of damp caves (*left*) in western Scotland. By robbing travelers on the coastal road near Ballantrae, Sawney and his partner grew rich in everything except what mattered – food. Faced with starvation, they had taken to eating their victims (*above*)!

When it was finally discovered, the cave was sheltering a clan of cannibal children. The clan was later executed in Edinburgh, Scotland.

LONGBOW HOTSHOTS
Today, Robin Hood is known for his deadly shot with the longbow. In fact, when the Robin Hood legend began, longbows were little used. They begin to appear in legal records as a favorite weapon of robbers from the mid-13th century onward. Later, they played a vital role in England's victories at Crécy (1346, page 20) and Agincourt (1415).

The longbow was much cheaper than a crossbow (*left*). It was quicker and easier to use, too, but needed great skill to be used effectively.

Welsh archers kept their rear foot bare to prevent slipping (right). They could pierce armor at 100 paces with a well-aimed arrow.

THE AGE OF THE BRIGAND

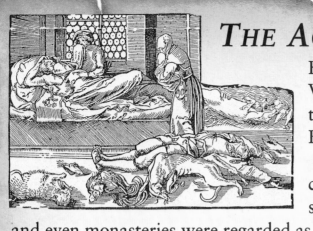

For much of the 14th and 15th centuries, Western Europe was overrun by brigands. They took advantage of the disruption caused by the Black Plague, and the almost constant wars.

Huge groups of bandits roamed the countryside – outlaws, vagrants, thugs, and ex-soldiers of every description. Villages, towns, and even monasteries were regarded as targets.

The chronicler Froissart was one of the first to use the word "brigand" for these thugs. He was describing soldiers in the reign of John II of France who fell into the worst excesses of banditry. Another group of French bandits was the "false pilgrims," or *coquillards*, named after the emblem of a pilgrim's shell which they used to deceive their victims. Germany was plagued by *raubritter*, or "thieving knights." In Spanish Catalonia, armies of brigands sieged towns, while Italy suffered from roving mercenary knights, or *condottieri* (*main picture*).

THE 100 YEARS' WAR

The 100 Years' War rumbled on between England (whose flag is *left*), Burgundy, and France from 1337 to 1453. Bloody campaigns, decided by tortuous sieges and fierce battles (like Crécy, 1346, *below*), were separated by short periods of peace.

The warring countries had to contend with the miseries of war – loss of life, destruction, high taxation, and danger from marauding gangs of ill-disciplined soldiers.

FALSTAFF. In his play *Henry IV, Part I*, William Shakespeare suggests how easy highway robbery was before there were police forces. Short of cash, the rogue knight Sir John Falstaff (*left*) makes a night attack on travelers at Gad's Hill in Kent, England. Wearing a disguise, he steals their money, but is robbed by his friends (including Prince Henry). Later, when told what had happened, Falstaff pretends he recognized his attackers, but chose not to hurt them. "Was it for me to kill the heir apparent?" He lies!

A walled town – many towns and villages in this era fortified themselves against brigand attacks.

Mercenaries (above) *were a menace well into the 17th century, as shown in this raid in 1612.*

A Landsknecht, the 16th century's most feared mercenary.

GREAT COMPANIES OF BRIGANDS

Companies of mercenaries were a major problem in late medieval times. One such band, the English White Company of Sir John Hawkwood, fought in Italy. If the Company was regularly paid, it was a useful ally. But when no wages were paid, it deteriorated into a bandit gang and that was a danger to friend and foe.

PUNISHMENT AND LAW

A rare sight – highwaymen repairing the roads. Most were hung once caught.

Medieval society was divided between peasants and a comparatively small number of landowners and wealthy merchants. The privileged few feared banditry because it threatened to overturn the established order.

Rulers made laws that protected their interests. Methods of trial were crude, and torture was widespread. Horrific punishments, such as boiling and lashing alive (slicing off the skin), were designed to deter criminals. But they could never deter those bandits who made a living by crime – or died of starvation. Yet up to the 19th century, the penalty for robbery remained death.

CONFESS – OR DIE

Suspects were tortured to get information about other criminals, or to make them confess. Victims in extreme pain often confessed to crimes they had not done, just to stop the torture!

Tortures included gouging out eyes, and stretching on the rack, which slowly dislocated arms and legs. Victims were also dropped into water (*above*). They were forced under until they confessed to their crimes.

A 17th-century thumbscrew

Trial by Fire

In the triple ordeal by fire (below), suspects walked nine feet carrying a 3-pound lump of red-hot iron. The wound was bound and left for three days. If burn marks remained when it was unwrapped, the accused was declared guilty.

FINGERS AND TOES

Hands and feet were a torturer's favorite targets. Thumbscrews crushed fingers, so they could never be used again.

The "boot" was a large metal shoe. The victim's foot was placed inside and the boot was tightened with screws, grinding the foot to a pulp. Many prisoners told their captors what they wanted to hear before the tightening began.

I've Got a Crush on You

Today, suspects can plead "Not Guilty." But in the 17th century the accused had to plead guilty before a trial went ahead. Those refusing to plead were crushed by weights (peine forte et dure) until admitting guilt – or dying.

An 18th-Century Prison
No place for the weak!

CHEAP PUNISHMENT!

Today the most common punishment for serious crimes is imprisonment.

But up to the 19th century, prison was rarely used for the poor, because it was expensive. The authorities preferred quicker, cheaper punishments.

The simplest were execution or cutting off a hand or foot. For lesser crimes, the *pillory* or *stocks* were used.

Torture was officially abolished in the 1620s, but terrible prison conditions may have made prisoners wonder if it was true (*left*)!

THE POET BANDITS

Among the most romantic bandits were Christian Greek rebels known as *klephts*. Their name came from the Greek word *kleptes*, meaning a thief. It has the same origin as our word for a compulsive thief – *kleptomaniac*.

The klephts date from the 15th century, when Greece was conquered by troops of the Turkish Ottoman Empire. Bands of Greeks took to the hills and woods (*above*) to continue their struggle against the invader. There they gathered into tribes, each with its own distinctive culture, that survived for centuries.

The life of the klephts focused on war, games, poetry, and drinking. Many maintained a strict standard, robbing only Muslims and the rich. The lively ballads in which they recorded their adventures are still famous today.

OTTOMAN EMPIRE (c.1560)

EUROPE — Vienna • — ASIA
Danube R. — Constantinople — **KLEPHT REGION**
Mediterranean Sea — PERSIA
Cairo • — Basra •
AFRICA — Nile R. — ARABIA

THE OTTOMAN EMPIRE

The principal enemies of the Christian klephts were the Muslim Turks of the Ottoman Empire. Beginning at a base in central Turkey in the early 14th century, the Ottomans gradually conquered a vast empire (see map, *above*).

At its height, it reached from the gates of Vienna in the west to Basra in the east. By the 19th century, however, Ottoman power was in decline. Some territories were lost to other major powers. Others, such as Greece, fought successfully for independence.

A Klepht Symposium (right). *This was a party at which klephts (mostly the men) ate, drank, talked, and danced long into the night. They loved to hear tales of the past, and a good storyteller was as respected as a mighty warrior.*

The Capture of Constantinople (right). By this time (1456) most of Greece was already in Turkish hands.

Patriotic Fighters?
In theory the Turks were the klephts' main enemy, but it was often Greek peasants who suffered most from klepht raids.

On some occasions, peasants even asked the Turks to protect them from the brigands!

TAME KLEPHTS

The hostility between the Turks and the klephts lasted for three centuries. On many occasions the Turks sent powerful forces to destroy the bandits. They never succeeded because the klephts usually fought with the support of the local people in countryside they knew intimately. Eventually, the Turks were forced to take some "tamed" klephts into government service, in the hope that they would help win over the others. The tactic was more successful than military confrontation!

HEROES...

In 1821, the Greeks living in the Ottoman provinces of the Danube and Morea rose against their Turkish masters. The following year, the entire Greek nation launched an all-out war on the Turks.

The klephts provided a ready-made fighting force, though bandit tactics were not always suited to a campaign. But by 1832, they had helped Greece achieve independence.

...OR VILLAINS?

Bandit leaders were partly attracted by the British gold paid to all those who fought for freedom. Many brigands also continued to plunder Greek peasants while fighting the Turks.

Greek rebels (above) of the 19th century, wearing the distinctive national dress.

STAND AND DELIVER!

Although travelers had been robbed on their journeys for centuries, the first highwaymen appeared in the late 17th century. They were the results of two developments – the growth of stagecoach traffic (first used in 1658) and the invention of the flintlock pistol (1683).

Of all countries, England was the highwayman's home, probably because the country was so poorly policed. During the 1640s, the army of King Charles I had been defeated in the Civil War. As a result, many young (and previously rich) horsemen were outlawed and turned to crime.

Soon, highwaymen stories abounded. They became the new Robin Hoods – heroic horsemen of the open road, carrying off fat purses and shapely ladies at will. Though many highwaymen were just vicious robbers, one remarkable fact remains – in an era when life was cheap, very few highwaymen ever killed their victims.

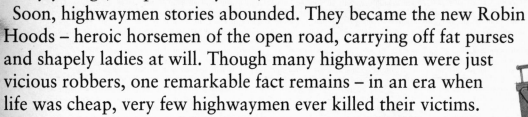

JACK SHEPPARD

Tiny highwayman Jack Sheppard (*above*) excelled at two things: getting caught and escaping! Five times he was arrested and four times he escaped. His breakouts, helped by his girlfriend "Edgeworth Bess," became legendary.

After his final escape, Jack strutted about London bragging of his exploits. He was arrested and bound with heavy chains weighing 265 lbs. Two weeks later, the play *Harlequin Jack Sheppard* appeared. The legend had begun...

The Flintlock
Before the 17th century, guns were fired by lit fuses, which meant that the user could never be quite sure when the weapon was going to fire.

The flintlock struck flint against steel, sending a shower of sparks onto the priming powder, causing the gun to go off.

"YOUR MONEY OR YOUR LIFE!"

The famous cries of the highwayman were "Stand and deliver!" and "Your money or your life!" (*below*). The English were strangely proud of their highwaymen. They showed delighted fascination when one of them managed to rob King George I of his watch and money in his own yard!

In the United States, highwaymen were known as "Road Agents." One of the earliest was Michael Martin, alias "Captain Lightfoot." Martin was as gallant as any in Europe, but he was caught and hanged in 1822.

THE WICKED LADIES. Mary Frith (1584–1659), known as Moll Cutpurse, was such a famous thief that the play *The Roaring Girl* (1611) was based on her life while she was still on the loose! Regarded by some historians as the first true highway robber, she was a highly skilled rider who only held up opponents of King Charles I!

Lady Catherine Ferrers was a landowner's wife who robbed coaches just for the thrill of it (the film *The Wicked Lady* was based on her life). After many daring holdups, she was finally shot by one of her victims. Her amazing life added to the romantic image of the elegant thief robbing in the moonlight (*top*).

A HIGHWAYMAN'S LAST HOLDUP

The penalty for highway robbery was death by hanging (*right*). Because of the severity of the punishment, juries were often unwilling to convict. Before the creation of the Horse Patrol in 1805, the highwaymen's chief danger was bounty hunters after the $80 reward for their capture.

DICK TURPIN

No highwayman is more famous than Dick Turpin (*left*). In numerous stories, ballads, and movies he is the ideal "gentleman of the road" – a handsome figure on his noble mare, Black Bess, dashing along the highways, robbing the greedy of their money, and the women of their hearts.

The real Richard Turpin was nothing at all like this. He was a butcher by trade, 5 feet 9 inches tall with a pock-marked face. He did not have a horse named Black Bess, nor did he make a famous ride from London to York to escape capture. He stole from both rich and poor, and rather than wooing women, he tortured them.

Born in 1706, Turpin gave up his butcher's business in favor of poaching and burglary. In time, he became a murderer and highway robber with a reward of $120 for his capture. He was eventually caught when his writing was identified, and he was hanged at York in 1739.

TURPIN LEAPS THE TOLLGATE

Legend says that Dick Turpin rode his mare, Black Bess, from London to York in twelve hours (main picture, *right*). Exhausted by the ride, the horse died just before reaching their destination. This supposedly impossible feat gave Turpin the perfect alibi for a robbery he had committed.

This story is an excellent example of how facts become confused. The marathon ride to York was first attributed to "Swift John Nevison." A report from 1676 claims Nevison carried out a robbery at Gad's hill in Kent at 4:00 A.M., then rode to York by 7:45 P.M. that evening.

THE BEGGAR'S OPERA. The romantic hero of John Gay's *Beggar's Opera* (1728) is Macheath, highwayman, robber, and womanizer (*left*). This ever-popular musical illustrates perfectly the English people's sympathetic attitude toward their highwaymen.

In 1773, angry magistrates called for the show to be banned!

JONATHAN WILD

Jonathan Wild (*left*) was the craftiest criminal of his age. Titled the "Thief-taker General of Great Britain and Ireland," he lived by catching criminals for reward and selling back to people their stolen property.

Yet it was Wild who organized the robberies, and the villains he handed over had refused to obey him! In the end, the law caught up with Wild and he was hanged at Tyburn, London in 1739.

Blueskin Blake, a London criminal, was so furious at "Judas" Wild for betraying him that he tried to cut the Thief-taker's throat (above, right).

Frenchman Claude Duval (right) *certainly pretended to be a gentleman of the road, dressing and speaking with great style. He was irresistible to women.*

It is reported that in the middle of a holdup, he took time to dance with a lady on Hounslow Heath, (near London, below left)! Sadly, he performed his final dance on the end of a hangman's rope.

GENTLEMEN OF THE ROAD

A few highwaymen were genuine "gentlemen of the road." These were generally bankrupt young men who turned to crime to restore their fortunes.

Two famous gentlemen highwaymen were Old Etonian William Parsons and James Maclaine, a minister's son.

After a dissolute life, including some rather amateur highway robbery, Parsons was executed for running away from a penal colony. Maclaine conducted a number of brave but non-violent robberies before he too was caught and executed.

ROB ROY

Scotland has provided many famous bandit stories. For centuries the government had great difficulty policing the rugged countryside, dominated by clans whose first loyalty was to themselves. The situation was not helped by ceaseless raiding and counter-raiding over the border with England, and by English interference in Scottish affairs (*left*).

Rob Roy Macgregor, the Robin Hood of the glens, is the best known of all Scottish bandits. A cattle grazer in the Highlands, he and his followers were driven to cattle-stealing by the activities of Highland bandits. In 1691, he joined the Jacobites – those who wanted the Stuarts restored to the thrones of Scotland and England.

By 1716, following the failure of a Jacobite rising, Rob Roy was a full-fledged outlaw. From this time come the stories of his generosity toward the poor, and fantastic escapes. Captured in 1727, he was pardoned and died seven years later.

THE FICTIONAL OUTLAW. The Scottish novelist Sir Walter Scott brought Rob Roy international fame as the central figure of his novel *Rob Roy* (1817). Scott took liberties with history. He romanticized the rough, kilted Highlanders and belittled the English redcoats. His readers loved the formula, and since then it has been the inspiration for many books, and a movie starring Liam Neeson (*above*).

THE BORDER RAIDERS

Scotland's border with England is a lonely place of bleak hillsides and swiftly-flowing rivers. Granite castles (such as Craigivar, *left*, and Kildrummy, *below*) stand as a grim reminder that this was perfect bandit country.

Banditry was a way of life there for many centuries. Robbers and cattle thieves fought running battles with each other, and with the authorities. King after king attempted to bring control to the region without success.

The many ballads of famous characters were first collected by Sir Walter Scott in his *Minstrelsy of the Scottish Border* (1802–03).

King Robert II (above) came to the Scottish throne in 1390. An invalid with few kingly qualities, he maintained a weak government in which laws were increasingly ignored.

THE GREAT CLAN BATTLE

One of Robert's most poorly planned attempts to stamp out violence came in 1396. Tired of the endless squabbling between Clan Chattan and Clan Kay, the king invited them to settle their differences in an organized battle. In a specially marked area, thirty Chattans and thirty Kays fought to the death. After twenty-nine Kays had been slain, the Chattans were declared the victors. The real loser, however, was law and order.

The End of the Clans
The constant feuding between the clans was only halted by a crushing defeat at the Battle of Culloden in 1746 (right).

The clans had flocked to the side of Bonnie Prince Charlie in his bid to win back the English Crown, but defeat led to the destruction of the clan system.

SMUGGLERS

Smugglers were the least feared of all bandits. Although smuggling attracted some vicious characters, they generally did not harm other people. Their enemy was the government, and in particular customs officers (*left*).

The British government taxed imported foreign luxuries, such as tobacco, alcohol, and tea, which were popular but not essential. Even so, the taxes hit the poor harder than the rich. In other countries, such as pre-Revolutionary France, taxes fell on essential goods such as salt. Such taxes were hated, especially by the poor.

Even in the 20th century, prohibition in the United States led to a wave of smuggling. Whatever was taxed, there were always men and women who were prepared to smuggle to avoid paying. And since the poor were least able to pay, in their eyes these smugglers were heroes!

Tea Smugglers (below) *wore special jackets under their clothes.*

The Smuggler's Haunt
No smuggler could operate effectively without a good place to hide their goods. Caves provided a perfect hiding place, such as these on the Gower coastline in England (above).

THE SAME THE WORLD OVER
Smuggling took place all over the world, and not just along the coasts. Many goods, such as tea in China and salt in France, were taxed as they were moved around the country. French merchants also smuggled tobacco (*right*) and brandy to England.

Tea smuggling was big business in 19th century China, attracting huge gangs, some several thousand strong.

Cap.t James Carrington's
Best, Mild York-River Tobacco,
LONDON.

Smuggling Brandy
In 18th-century England the tax on brandy was 16 shillings a barrel. Since it could be bought in France for 16 shillings, the tax doubled its price.

A SMUGGLER'S SONG. The romantic image of the smuggler as a trader who brought benefit to the whole community is captured in this extract from Rudyard Kipling's poem *A Smuggler's Song*:

Five and twenty ponies,
Trotting through the dark
Brandy for the Parson,
'Baccy [tobacco] for the Clerk;
Laces for a lady, letters for a spy,
And watch the wall, my darling, while the Gentlemen go by!

HIDING THE LOOT

Government officers were always on the lookout for smugglers, which led to their adopting all sorts of tricks to make sure their precious cargoes came safely ashore.

One device was to hide barrels in the sea, weighing them down and marking their position with a float. Like this, they looked like fishermen's crab pots and could be collected when the coast was clear (*top*). Another method was to place a tin lining inside barrels, so that cigars could be hidden.

PROHIBITION

In 1920, the United States amended its constitution to ban the manufacture and sale of alcoholic beverages. This act was a complete failure. Alcohol was made illegally (*right*), and was smuggled in from abroad. Bootleggers distributed it for huge profits. The ban ended in 1933.

THE FATE OF DANIEL CHATER

Daniel Chater was a poor shoemaker from England. The surrounding region was terrorized by the Hawkhurst Gang, a band of dastardly smugglers who traded with the French (*left*).

In 1748, the gang raided a customs house and stole quantities of brandy and tea. Chater knew one of the gang, John Diamond, and decided to claim a large reward by giving his name to the authorities. Chater and lawman William Galley then traveled to give evidence at Diamond's trial. Foolishly, they spent the night at an inn. The gang found out where they were, seized them, and led them out into the countryside. After being mercilessly beaten, Galley was buried alive, and Chater was thrown down a well (*main picture*).

THE TERRIBLE WRECKERS

Wreckers were a mariner's worst enemy. Waiting for a stormy night, when the moon and stars were not visible, they chose a dangerous stretch of coast and replaced the normal navigation lights with false lights of their own.

Unsuspecting vessels were drawn onto the rocks and shipwrecked. The wreckers swarmed down to the shore. Gathering up whatever valuables they could lay their hands on, they fled inland before the law arrived to guard the ship.

Buried Alive!
*Not all smugglers were
people just trying to make a
bit of money on the side.*
*After throwing Chater down
the well, the Hawkhurst Gang
piled stones on top of him
until he stopped screaming.
Their leader, Thomas
Kingsmill, was
hanged the
next year.*

THE REVENUE OFFICERS

Smuggling could be stopped only by
patrolling all coasts and rivers. One reason
it was not stamped out was because the
authorities were not prepared to pay
for sufficient law officers to do this.
"We are very much infested with
smugglers," wrote one despairing
customs officer in 1740. "Several...
have called at my house, swearing
they would kill me or any
other officer they should
meet with... I humbly beg
we may be supplied with
some soldiers."
None were sent,
and the smugglers
continued their
illegal trade.

"Creepers"
*These grapels (above) were used
by the customs officers to find
sunken goods. They were
dragged along the seabed in
small rowboats.*

John Pixley
(left) *was a
customs officer
who became a
smuggler.*

Dr. Syn. Few writers have done
more to build up the romantic
image of the smuggler than
novelist Russel Thorndyke.
His seven thrilling smuggling stories are
set on the lonely marshes of England. They
feature the extraordinary Dr. Syn, a wayward
minister, friend of the Prince Regent, scholar, and
daredevil smuggler!
Visitors to the area may stay in the famous
Mermaid Inn, once a refuge of the real-life Hawkhurst
Gang. They can even stay in "Dr. Syn's Bedroom,"
complete with its genuine secret passage (*right*), hidden
behind a false bookshelf!

Smugglers' Cottages
*These often contained
secret rooms for
hiding smuggled
goods from revenue
officers.*

THE WILD WEST

In most people's minds the word "bandit" immediately conjures up images of the "Wild West." This is not because the West was particularly wild, but because its banditry has been made famous by writers and the Hollywood filmmakers (*left*).

In God-fearing, small-town early America banditry was comparatively rare. However, it did flourish in the decades following the Civil War (1861-1865). When settlers moved into the open spaces west of the Mississippi, the rule of law was often slow to follow the wagon train. It is wrong to think that bandits lurked behind every hill, but writers realized that this is just what the city dwellers in the East wanted to read about. So the myth of the Wild West was born (*below*).

AN ECCENTRIC ROBBER

Charles E. Bolton, known as "Black Bart," prided himself on never spilling a drop of blood and robbing only coach companies. He was distinguished by his educated accent, the sack he wore over his head (cut with two eye holes), and the poetry he left in the boxes he had just robbed! He was eventually caught when a detective traced the laundry mark "F.O.X. 7" on a handkerchief Black Bart had left behind at the scene of the crime.

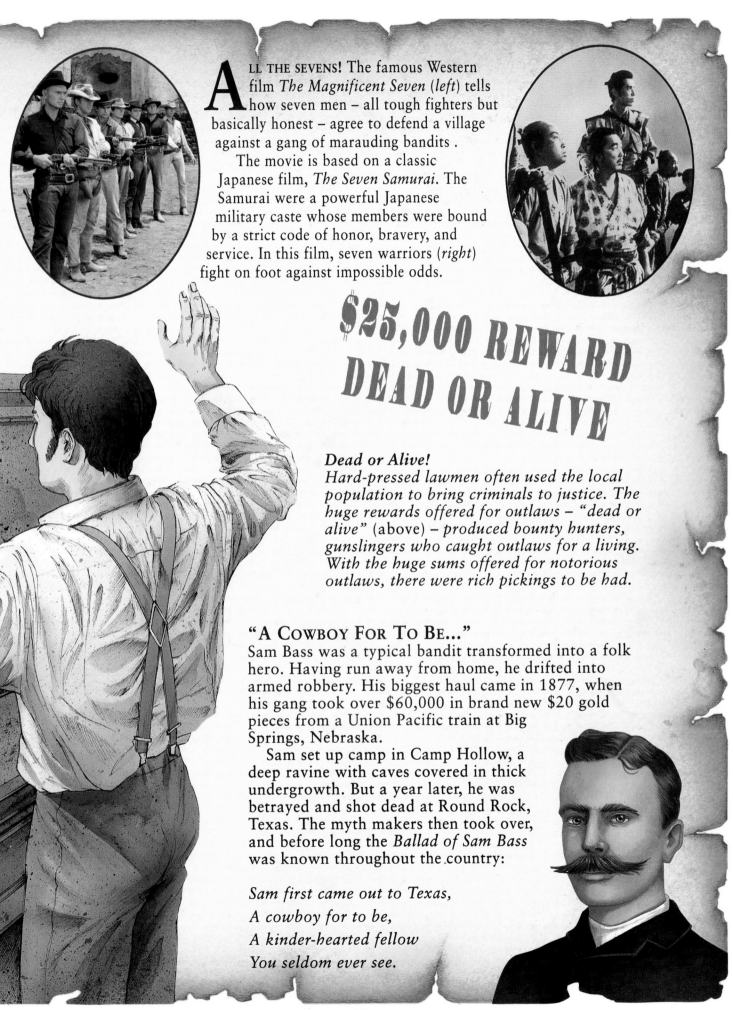

ALL THE SEVENS! The famous Western film *The Magnificent Seven* (left) tells how seven men – all tough fighters but basically honest – agree to defend a village against a gang of marauding bandits .

The movie is based on a classic Japanese film, *The Seven Samurai*. The Samurai were a powerful Japanese military caste whose members were bound by a strict code of honor, bravery, and service. In this film, seven warriors (right) fight on foot against impossible odds.

$25,000 REWARD DEAD OR ALIVE

Dead or Alive!
Hard-pressed lawmen often used the local population to bring criminals to justice. The huge rewards offered for outlaws – "dead or alive" (above) – produced bounty hunters, gunslingers who caught outlaws for a living. With the huge sums offered for notorious outlaws, there were rich pickings to be had.

"A Cowboy For To Be..."
Sam Bass was a typical bandit transformed into a folk hero. Having run away from home, he drifted into armed robbery. His biggest haul came in 1877, when his gang took over $60,000 in brand new $20 gold pieces from a Union Pacific train at Big Springs, Nebraska.

Sam set up camp in Camp Hollow, a deep ravine with caves covered in thick undergrowth. But a year later, he was betrayed and shot dead at Round Rock, Texas. The myth makers then took over, and before long the *Ballad of Sam Bass* was known throughout the country:

Sam first came out to Texas,
A cowboy for to be,
A kinder-hearted fellow
You seldom ever see.

JESSE JAMES

On April 3, 1882, a killer died and a hero was born – Jesse Woodson James, known as "Dingus" to his friends.

As a slim, handsome 15-year-old, Jesse rode with Confederate leader Charles Quantrill (*left*) in the Civil War. He learned how to steal horses – and kill in cold blood. In 1866, Jesse robbed his first bank. Seven years later his gang held up their first train, stealing some $2,000.

The gang proceeded to rob and shoot its way to national fame, once holding up two stage coaches in a day. Eventually, with a $10,000 reward on his head, Jesse was killed by a shot in the head.

Like the barons of Robin Hood's day, the banks and railroad companies were popular targets, and legend soon made a star of the daring young Jesse. By the close of the 19th century, already the subject of over 270 novels, he was firmly established as an American legend.

The railroads are the enemy of poor farmers in many Wild West stories (left), and thus are a fair target for outlaws.

THE POWER OF LEGEND. To some, Jesse James will always be the dashing youth outwitting his pursuers and fighting against injustice.

The reality is rather different. Jesse was undoubtedly brave, but he was also a cruel and violent man. For 16 years his gang survived by bullying weak officials and depending on the support of relatives to hide them. There is no firm evidence that he ever gave money to anyone in need, or that he fought for the oppressed.

Bandits and Cowboys
In the legendary Wild West, cowboys are glamorous figures who devote themselves to the fight against bandits (left).
But the real cowboys were merely cattle drovers, not high-minded amateur lawmen. Few cowboys even wore a gun!

GOOD-BYE, JESSE!

Bob Ford shot Jesse James as he was straightening a picture at his home in St. Joseph, Kansas. "The gun went off accidentally," he muttered to Jesse's wife, but he still claimed the reward. Jesse's death was front-page news all over the country (*right*). The inscription on the post over his grave read:

*Jesse W. James
Died April 3, 1882
Aged 34 years, 6 months, 28 days
Murdered by a coward whose name is not worthy to appear here.*

Jesse James was said to have "invented" train robbery (above) — but in fact the Reno brothers of Indiana were the first.

GOOD BYE, JESSE!

The Notorious Outlaw and Bandit, Jesse James, Killed at St. Joseph

BY R. FORD, OF RAY COUNTY,

A Young Man but Twenty-one Years of Age.

THE DEADLY WEAPON USED

Presented to His Slayer by His Victim but a Short Time Since.

A ROBBERY CONTEMPLATED

Of a Bank at Platte City—To Have Taken Place Last Night.

JESSE IN KANSAS CITY

During the Past Year and Residing on One of the Principal Streets.

KANSAS CITY EXCITED

Over the Receipt of the News—Talks with People— Life of the Dead Man.

"PULL THIS TRAIN UP!"

On June 2, 1899, the driver of the Union Pacific Overland Flyer saw a red lantern ahead. Two men jumped aboard and ordered him to separate the passenger cars, and move the train forward.

He refused. "Pull this train up!" the bandit snapped. Refusing again, the driver was beaten. The robbers drove the train themselves, and once over a nearby bridge, blew the safe. Minutes later, Butch Cassidy and the Sundance Kid made their getaway, richer by $30,000!

BANDITS COME TO TOWN! Buffalo Bill's Wild West Show helped spread the myth of the Wild West around the world (*left*). To begin with, he put on costume exhibitions. But realizing that his audiences wanted more action, he staged mock fights between cowboys and indians, and even bandit holdups of trains and stagecoaches.

AUSTRALIA'S BUSHRANGERS

Australia's most feared bandits were the bushrangers. Their history is divided into two parts. The first bushrangers were convicts who escaped into the bush (the Australian wilderness) from the penal settlements. They survived by robbing farmers, gold merchants, and travelers with the cry, "Bail up!"

Some of the poorer Australians felt sorry for the bushrangers and helped them in whatever ways they could, often informing them of police movements.

The second phase of bushranging came later, when native Australians fled from the police and took refuge in the bush as outlaws. Among such men were Ben Hall, who was surrounded and riddled with 15 bullets in 1865.

This phase is also famous for the exploits of Ned Kelly (see page 42), who was the most famous bushranger of all.

CRIMINAL COLONIES

The English began sentencing criminals to transportation to Australian penal colonies in 1788. Before long, they were the most popular dumping ground for the country's unwanted villains.

Life in the penal settlements "down under" was horrible. Criminals were poorly housed, clothed, and fed. They worked long hours, often in chain gangs, and were severely punished for the smallest offenses (*above left*).

Daylight Robbery!
Bushrangers held up Chinese laborers on the highway leading to gold mines (below). Gold was discovered in 1851 and from then on the gold mines were always a popular target for bandit attacks.

Famous bushrangers from this period included Dan Morgan, Harry Power, and "Captain Thunderbolt."

BLACK TRACKERS
Aboriginal Australians recruited into the police force were known as Black Trackers (*below*). Their local knowledge, toughness, and remarkable scouting skills made them the bushrangers' most feared opponents.

Other Aboriginal Australians became bushrangers, often because of harsh treatment by the police. The most famous was Ben Hall, who conducted a three-year reign of terror in the province of New South Wales.

BUSHRANGING POWER
Harry Power, born in Ireland, was transported in 1840 to Tasmania, Australia, for robbing a bank. In 1855, he was sentenced to 14 years for wounding a policeman after an argument.

Escaping from Pentridge prison, he began bushranging in Victoria. He quickly acquired a reputation as a colorful but harmless rogue. But, in 1870, he was sent to prison after being betrayed by a comrade. Before he was caught, he took on a young apprentice named Ned Kelly (see page 42).

Good Timing!
Power was even said to have kept to highway robbing appointments made in advance (right)!

THE IRON BUSHRANGER

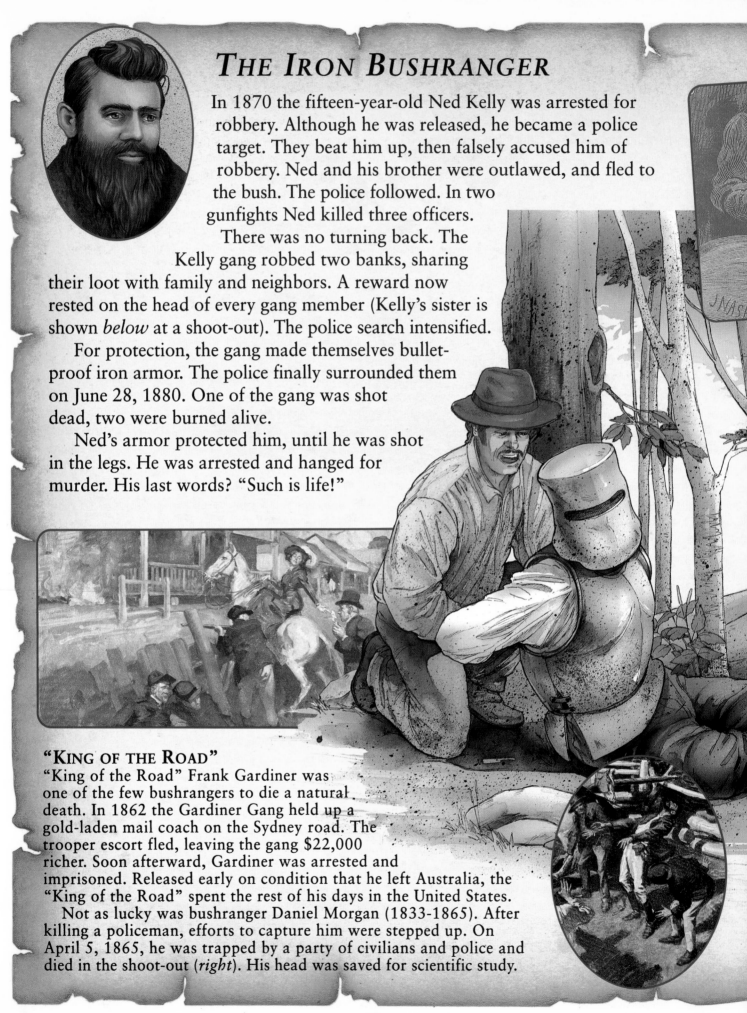

In 1870 the fifteen-year-old Ned Kelly was arrested for robbery. Although he was released, he became a police target. They beat him up, then falsely accused him of robbery. Ned and his brother were outlawed, and fled to the bush. The police followed. In two gunfights Ned killed three officers.

There was no turning back. The Kelly gang robbed two banks, sharing their loot with family and neighbors. A reward now rested on the head of every gang member (Kelly's sister is shown *below* at a shoot-out). The police search intensified.

For protection, the gang made themselves bullet-proof iron armor. The police finally surrounded them on June 28, 1880. One of the gang was shot dead, two were burned alive.

Ned's armor protected him, until he was shot in the legs. He was arrested and hanged for murder. His last words? "Such is life!"

"KING OF THE ROAD"

"King of the Road" Frank Gardiner was one of the few bushrangers to die a natural death. In 1862 the Gardiner Gang held up a gold-laden mail coach on the Sydney road. The trooper escort fled, leaving the gang $22,000 richer. Soon afterward, Gardiner was arrested and imprisoned. Released early on condition that he left Australia, the "King of the Road" spent the rest of his days in the United States.

Not as lucky was bushranger Daniel Morgan (1833-1865). After killing a policeman, efforts to capture him were stepped up. On April 5, 1865, he was trapped by a party of civilians and police and died in the shoot-out (*right*). His head was saved for scientific study.

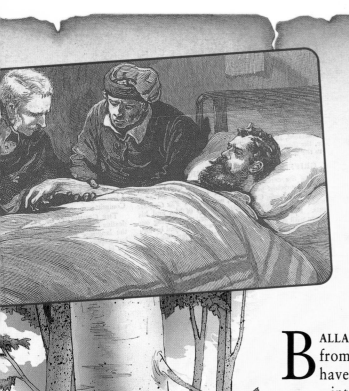

AUSTRALIA'S ROBIN HOOD?

Ned Kelly is Australia's number one bandit hero. His popularity rests on three things: the armor he wore in his last battle, his distribution of stolen wealth among relatives and friends, and the unjust way he was treated by the police as a young man. The picture on the left shows a typically sympathetic view of Kelly – the doctor finding 23 wounds in his leg.

But Ned is not everyone's hero. He was a thief, and he did shoot policemen (although he argued self defense). History's verdict is unproven. The Australian people's is not: Ned Kelly is their Robin Hood.

BALLADS have often whitewashed the brutal deeds of outlaws from Dick Turpin to Sam Bass. Some Australian ballads have likewise transformed the crimes of the bushrangers into acts of bravery, loyalty, and generosity. Even in pictures of the time (*below*), the robberies were sometimes shown as pranks rather than as acts of violence.

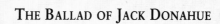

THE BALLAD OF JACK DONAHUE

Jack Donahue was an Irishman sentenced to transportation in 1824. He soon escaped and became a bushranger. Twice he was recaptured and escaped. Eventually, he was shot by a police sergeant:

Nine rounds the sergeant fired before the
fatal ball

Had lodged in the breast of O'Donahue
and caused him for to fall.

Before he closed his weary eyes he slowly bid
adieu,

Saying, "Good people all, both great and
small, say a prayer for John Donahue."

The Capture of Ned Kelly (from a Ballad)
"You can't hurt me!" mocked the iron-clad Ned Kelly.
A shotgun blast in the legs soon proved him wrong.

THE END OF THE BANDIT?

The 19th century saw a new type of bandit. This was the guerrilla, fighting for a political cause. They included the Spanish guerrillas of the Peninsular War, Mexican bandits like Zapata (depicted on screen by Marlon Brando, *left*) and African freedom fighters, such as Kenyan Mau Mau of the 1950s and the soldiers of the African National Congress.

Meanwhile, old-fashioned banditry declined. The bushrangers, outlaws, and highwaymen were brigands of the open countryside. Gradually, as the world population increased and more people became suburban dwellers, so banditry dwindled. It was also affected by more efficient policing.

Nevertheless, banditry has not disappeared completely. It survives in remote parts of Asia, Africa, and South America. In some areas it is connected with the drug trade. There are also car bandits who prey off unsuspecting tourists, rather like the highwaymen of the past. Perhaps, after all, the end of the bandit is still a long way off?

Guerrillas are unconventional soldiers who harass enemy forces with ambushes and sabotage. The original guerrillas were Spanish bandit gangs, helped by regular soldiers, who preyed off occupying French forces at the time of Napoleon I.

The bandits accounted for a quarter of all French casualties. In revenge, the French executed anyone suspected of helping the gangs (above).

ZAPATA – THE MEXICAN SAVIOR

Emiliano Zapata (1877–1919, *below left*) is Mexico's greatest guerrilla-hero. In 1911 he led a popular revolt against the tyrannical rule of Porfirio Diaz. His slogan was "Land and Liberty" – land for the native Mexicans who had lost their farms to immigrant Spaniards, and liberty for all citizens.

After initial success, by 1915 Zapata was in retreat. Four years later he was assassinated at Pueblo. To this day, many Mexicans believe that when things are really bad, Zapata will return to save them. Today's Zapatista movement (*below*) keeps alive the spirit of popular revolt in Mexico.

THE URBAN BANDITS

Beginning in medieval Sicily as a secret bandit gang, the Mafia spread from the countryside into the towns, and became involved in a wide variety of crime.

Today the organization is also powerful in the United States, where it is known as *Cosa Nostra*, "Our Business." It is organized into families, each with an all-powerful boss (*capo*). The Mafia has stakes in activities like gambling, protection rackets, drug smuggling, and prostitution.

Secrecy, loyalty, and ferocious intimidation tactics make the Mafia members very hard to bring to justice.

Sicilian police scour the countryside looking for Mafia members (above).

BONNIE PARKER AND CLYDE BARROW formed a gang and indulged in a two-year spree of robbery and murder in the 1930s. Finally shot dead at a police roadblock, Bonnie and Clyde live on in songs and films (*above*).

DRUG BANDITS

Drug manufacturers in the "Golden Triangle" (the border of Myanmar, Laos, and Thailand) weigh their deadly product (opium) before smuggling it abroad for vast reward.

Massive demand for illegal drugs in the late 20th century has created bandit gangs of enormous wealth, power, and ferocity.

THE BANDIT WORLD

The map below shows where all the outlaws mentioned in this book came from. However, many other bandits and outlaws, not as famous but just as vicious, have operated throughout history in most countries of the world.

United States (1)
Road Agents (page 27), Wild West outlaws (page 36), Jesse James (page 38), Sam Bass (page 37), Black Bart (page 36), and prohibition smugglers (page 33).

England (2)
Robin Hood (page 18), highwaymen (page 26), Moll Cutpurse (page 27), Dick Turpin (page 28), smugglers (page 32), and Daniel Chater (page 34).

Scotland (3)
Sawney Bean (page 19), Rob Roy (page 30), and clan raiders (page 31).

France (4)
Clotild and Basina (page 16).

Greece (5)
Klephts (page 24).

China (6)
Huang Ch'ao (page 10), Outlaws of the Marsh (page 12), and Dzungarian raiders (page 9).

Mexico (7)
Bandits (page 44), Zapata (page 45), and the Zapatista movement (page 45).

Colombia (8)
Drug barons (page 45).

Spain (9)
Peninsular War guerrillas (page 44).

Italy (10)
Spartacus (page 8), Bulla (page 9), Brigands (page 20), and the original Mafia (page 45).

Middle East (11)
Ali Baba's bandits (page 14), and Caravan bandits (page 15).

India (12)
Phoolan Devi (page 6), and Thugs (page 15).

Myanmar (13)
Drug bandits of the Golden Triangle (page 45).

Australia (14)
Bushrangers (page 40), and Ned Kelly (page 42).

BANDIT TIMELINE

73-71 BC Spartacus leads a slave revolt against the Roman authorities.

3rd century AD Bulla's gang rampages through Roman Italy.

589 AD Princesses Clotild and Basina hire a bandit gang to attack Abbess Leubovera.

880 Bandit Huang Ch'ao attempts to become China's emperor.

970-1279 Song Dynasty China, setting for *Outlaws of the Marsh* (*left*).

1096 People's Crusade marches across Europe, looting and murdering.

1170 Murder of Thomas à Becket in Canterbury Cathedral by four of Henry I's knights.

1239 First mention of "Robert Hood, outlaw," possibly the real Robin Hood.

1396 King Robert II's attempt to stop clan fighting ends in disaster.

14th-15th centuries Western Europe terrorized by brigands.

1410-1437 Sawney Bean and his cannibal clan terrorize the west coast of Scotland.

1456 Ottoman Turks capture Constantinople. The Greek klephts (*right*) take to the hills and begin the struggle against the Muslim invaders.

Mid-1500s The expansion of the Ottoman Empire into Arabia ends rule of nomadic tribes and reduces bandit activity in the region.

1650s Development of stagecoach and flintlock begins era of highwaymen (*left*).

1659 Death of Moll Cutpurse, "mother" of highwaymen.

1668 Claude Duval dances with one of his victims during a hold-up near London.

1676 English highwayman Swift John Nevison reportedly rides from Kent to York (about 250 miles) in 15 hours, 45 minutes.

1684 Death of Lady Catherine Ferrers, the "Wicked Lady."

18th-19th centuries Smuggling at its peak in England (*right*).

1716-1727 Rob Roy's reign as a Scottish outlaw.

1739 Dick Turpin hanged at York.

1746 Defeat at the Battle of Culloden ends the threat of the Scottish clans.

1748 Hawkhurst Gang brutally murder Daniel Chater in Kent.

1832 Greece achieves independence, aided by the bandit klephts.

1830s Thugs suppressed by the British government in India.

1851 Discovery of gold in Australia starts golden era of Bushrangers.

1865 End of American Civil War heralds start of "Wild West."

1878 Death of Sam Bass, "Robin Hood of Texas."

1880 Bushranger Ned Kelly captured and hanged after shoot-out (*bottom*).

1882 Bob Ford shoots Jesse James in the back.

20th century Rise of urban population sees bandit gangs like Mafia move from countryside into cities.

1911 Emiliano Zapata leads popular revolt in Mexico.

1920-33 Prohibition of alcoholic drinks in United States leads to wave of smuggling.

1930s Bonnie and Clyde's reign of terror in the American mid-West.

1980 Phoolan Devi leads a bandit gang in the hills of India.

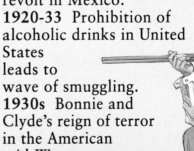

INDEX

Photographic credits *Abbreviations: t – top, m – middle, b – bottom, l – left, r – right.*
Cover, 13t, 14t, 16, 18t, 19tl & tr, 20m, 21, 23t, 24 all, 26t, 28t, 30t, 31, 32, 33t, 34b, 36m, 37, 38 both, 39, 40 both, 41 both: Mary Evans Picture Library; 4-5, 7, 17t, 20t & b, 23b, 25, 26b, 27 both, 30b, 44br: Hulton Deutsch Collection; 6t: Spectrum Colour Library; 6b, 8, 10b, 11 both, 12 both, 13b, 22, 28b, 45t & ml & b: Frank Spooner Pictures; 10t: Ancient Art & Architecture Collection; 14b, 34t, 35 both, 36t, 44t, 45 mr: Kobal Collection; 15: Bruce Coleman Ltd; 17b, 18b, 19m, 29b, 44bl: The Bridgeman Art Library; 29t & m, 33: Stewart Ross; 30: Roger Vlitos.